ARKANA

Sitting

Diana St. Ruth has practiced Buddhist meditation for many years, mainly in the Zen and Theravada traditions. She is currently editor of the British quarterly magazine, *Buddhism Now*. She organizes annual Buddhist summer schools and has written several books, including *The Little Book of Buddhist Wisdom*, *The Simple Guide to Zen Buddhism*, and *The Simple Guide to Theravada Buddhism*.

PENGUIN
ARKANA

a tricycle book

Sitting

A Guide to Buddhist Meditation

Diana St. Ruth

PENGUIN ARKANA

ARKANA

Published by the Penguin Group
Penguin Putnam Inc., 375 Hudson Street,
New York, New York 10014, U.S.A.
Penguin Books Ltd, 27 Wrights Lane,
London W8 5TZ, England
Penguin Books Australia Ltd, Ringwood,
Victoria, Australia
Penguin Books Canada Ltd, 10 Alcorn Avenue,
Toronto, Ontario, Canada M4V 3 B2
Penguin Books (N.Z.) Ltd, 182–190 Wairau Road,
Auckland 10, New Zealand

Penguin Books Ltd, Registered Offices:
Harmondsworth, Middlesex, England

First published in Great Britain under the title
Experience Beyond Thinking by
Buddhist Publishing Group 1993
First published in the United States of America
by Buddhist Publishing Group 1993
Published in a different format in Arkana 1998

10 9 8 7 6 5 4 3 2 1

Illustrations by Martha Ives

LIBRARY OF CONGRESS CATALOGING IN PUBLICATION DATA
St. Ruth, Diana.
  Sitting: a guide to Buddhist meditation/Diana St. Ruth.
    p.   cm.
  "A Tricycle book."
  ISBN 0 14 01.9568 8 (pbk.)
  1. Meditation—Buddhism.   2. Buddhism—Doctrines.   I. Title.
BQ5612.S7   1998
294.3´4435—dc21   97–37922

Printed in the United States of America
Set in Palatino
Designed by Virginia Norey

Dedicated to my brother John

contents

Introduction   xi

What Is Meditation?   1

Waking Up As If from a Dream   3

Experience Beyond Thinking   6

A Training?   9

The Purpose of Meditation   11

How to Meditate   13

Awareness   15

Awareness in Everyday Life   19

Sitting Meditation   20

The Lotus Posture   22

The Half Lotus   24

Simple Cross-legged Posture   25

Kneeling   26

Sitting on a Chair   27

Alternatives   28

The Spine   29

The Eyes   30

The Hands   31

Duration   32

When to Sit   34

Concentration   36

Counting Breaths   37

Subjects of Concentration   41

Alternative Subjects
of Concentration   43

Watch and Note Without Judging   45

The End of the Name   49

Nonattachment   51

Pain   53

Walking Meditation   55

In Review   61

Just Sit   65

Living Truth   69

The Unborn   71

Feel the Sensation   73

The Way   77

introduction

I used to have difficulty waking up in the morning and would consistently be late for work. A neighbor who knew of my problem presented me with an alarm clock for my twenty-first birthday. The alarm had a very large bell built into it that would raise the roof whenever it went off; then it would fall silent for a few seconds, and then off it would go again . . .

In the beginning it worked wonders, but after a little while my subconscious mind invented reasons for ignoring it. I began sometimes not to hear the alarm at all, loud as it was, or to convert the urgent sounds into something else.

Eventually, the day came, however, when I had to make a firm decision within myself to wake up when my alarm went off and to get to work on time, otherwise I was going to lose my job. As soon as the decision was made deep within myself, I did it.

Meditating is a bit like that; it is similar to arousing ourselves from a very deep sleep. We keep sleeping, dreaming beautiful dreams, or even suffering torments in horrendous nightmares—anything but waking up. We know it is time, but we don't really want to do it. We read books, listen to talks, think about what other people say, and yet don't actually do anything. We manage to convert all the information we gather into something that allows us to continue sleeping.

Do you want to wake up from the dream of life? Taking up meditation will be the deep decision within yourself that makes this possible.

Initially, meditation is a process of freeing the mind of its entanglements, of learning how to undo the knots. When I say "mind" here I mean mind and heart both, because the two are but one. When the mind is opened and the heart is softened, something begins to function that liberates one from the restricted world of the deluded mind.

Meditation is a way of being aware of everything experienced in life and also of recognizing the space in which life takes place; it is a process of becoming conscious of the obvious as well as the hidden.

Awareness is the key. But what does the word mean? To most people, perhaps, it denotes an acknowledgment of that which is going on around them in a general sort of way. In the context of meditation, however, it means "waking up," becoming acutely sensitive, knowing, feeling, living the moment in its pristine state, sensing colors and contours, sounds, textures, smells. It means recognizing tendencies within oneself yet resisting the pull to be controlled by them. This is meditation—to begin with at least.

Becoming aware of what happens deep within oneself may reveal the fact that there is very little real happiness there. Hoping, wishing, dreading—there may be plenty of that, but genuine happiness? . . .

Life is a bit of a game. We look forward to something and when it comes we criticize it, resent it, worry about it, want to change it, want to make it better.

For the most part, one's dreams are never fulfilled, and for the rest they are never quite right. I am talking now of the material world—the house, the car, the spouse, the children, the job; status, fun, security, health. It isn't a question of how much one has, but of how much real joy there is in it.

Why do I suffer? Is it the pain that makes me suffer? . . . the lack of food? . . . the lack of energy? . . . the lack of love? Is it oppression, dominance, the power of another that makes me suffer? Is it something out there? Or is it on the inside? Could it be that I suffer because of me?

The Buddha, a brave man, spoke the answer—he made the point clearly that whatever he said should not be taken as truth, but as an indicator, a signpost, a finger pointing to something beyond. "Each person," said the Buddha, "must realize and experience truth for himself or herself." Otherwise, what is it? Nothing but an idea, a useless concept floating in a sea of confusion. So the Buddha expressed what he experienced. "We suffer," he said, "from wanting what we do not already have." "Yes," you may say, "and what else?" Well, nothing else. That seems to be it. The cause of all suffering is yearning, wanting, wishing, desiring. It doesn't sound like much of a reason. What about the husband? . . . the wife? . . . the job? . . . the weather? What about the pain in my arm? What about the boy who committed suicide?

It sounds a bit glib to say they are what they are, but that is the truth of it. The boy committed suicide and any amount of wishing and wanting will not change that. The only thing I can change is my relationship to that fact. The decisions I have in life are related to how I live this moment, what I do and say now. I cannot change the past, arrange the future to suit myself, or make other people say and do the things I want them to say and do. All of my power is contained within this moment, related to this particular body and mind. This, however, is a very powerful position to be in.

There is no point in pondering a lot of "truths" and discussing them with others on an intellectual level without ever trying them out for yourself. The tendency may be to hesitate and procrastinate, put it all off until tomorrow, to talk and think about other people while never entering your own world. "Enlightenment has waited this long; it can wait one more day. In the meantime, I want to finish wallpapering the back bedroom, see that film, and get in touch with the mechanic about the terrible job he did on my car."

The time may come, however, when one more day is one day too long; when this life just isn't worth it anymore, and when the inspiration rises up in one's heart to step out of the old routine and into something completely new.

What is presented here in this small volume is drawn from my own experiences of Buddhist meditation practiced over a span of some twenty-odd years with numerous good and wise friends.

Anyone who wants to meditate can, but some have psychological needs that are not necessarily met by delving into the labyrinths of the mind unassisted. Do what is right for you.

Diana St. Ruth

Sitting

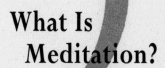

What Is
Meditation?

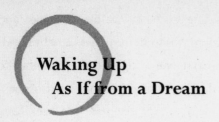

Waking Up
As If from a Dream

There are many methods of Buddhist meditation being taught throughout the world today, but my belief is that the Buddha himself didn't teach any method at all. He was a man who is said to have walked out on his beloved wife and small son, and on an entire kingdom (he was an Indian prince), in order to take to the road in rags without a penny to his name.

The Buddha turned his back on material comforts, on his family, on the priests, and even on the holy men he met along the way whose wisdom, he felt, did not reach the mark. He sat alone, accompanied merely by his own deep honesty and awareness, and refused to move until the barriers to truth were shattered.

His method (according to the *sutras*, the dialogues and discourses of the Buddha) was to sit in stillness and be mindfully aware, allowing first one thing and then another to arise and pass away, clinging to no experience whatsoever.

Over the centuries all sorts of elaborate practices have been devised—mantras, koans, visualizations, prostrations, chants, bows, and so on. These forms, rituals, and implements can be beautiful, helpful, true, and valid (I have certainly found them to be so), but they are not always the direct way of proceeding for everyone. And for some, they may even prove to be a diversion that could engage them for the rest of their lives to little advantage.

The point is, anything can be helpful. But if the effects are negative and the practices begin to use you, then something is not right.

Buddhism was never meant to be an "ism." One wonders what the man himself would have to say today if he saw what had grown up in his name. The Buddha laid great emphasis on encouraging others to look into themselves for themselves and to rely on that—something unborn, unmade, something beyond culture and creed and the value judgments of oneself and others.

The Buddha didn't really have a method other than awareness, and awareness is no method at all; it is a straightforward "opening of the eyes," a kind of waking up as if from a dream.

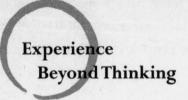

Experience
Beyond Thinking

I can look into your eyes and think about you, but not really see you. I can think about what it was like in the past for us and what it could be like in the future. When we live in the world with our minds full of thoughts, we don't sense much more than those thoughts; the focus of our attention is directed towards what is in the mind rather than what is in front of our faces.

Forms, at such times, are blurred and colors are dull. If we think about what we see, hear, smell, taste, and touch, instead of just seeing, hearing, smelling, tasting, and touching, we do not get the full flavor of the experience.

Try doing a job, any job, without thinking about the job itself or anything else. Simply stay with the body. Look at a pair of shoes and know them for what they are, resisting the temptation to form a mental image of them in your mind, or saying the word silently to yourself. Put the shoes on without telling yourself what you are doing. Stay with the process, the action in the body. Allow the action to do itself very naturally in the body. That is experience without thought, beyond thought; it is undistorted and unadulterated experience; nothing has been added to the process, and nothing has been taken away.

If I plunge my hands into steaming hot water, I don't need to think about whether the water is hot or not! I don't need to tell myself, "Oh! I've scalded my hands."

All situations are immediately known for what they are without the aid of thought. In fact, thinking usually only confounds the mind. So why do we do so much of it? Because we believe we have to, and because it is our habit to do so. With practice, however, we can learn to trust nature a little more. This is what we do in meditation.

Thinking is, of course, part of life too, and in certain forms it is invaluable. Wisely reflecting, skillfully planning, contemplating—these are creative forms of thought, but this is not the kind of thinking I am talking about, and it is not the sort most of us engage in most of the time. The majority of us, it seems to me, spend a good deal of our lives thinking about what has happened, or what is about to happen, and from time to time become attached to particular thought patterns that sap our strength and overshadow everything we do.

There I am driving along Baker Street on a Monday morning in the thick of the traffic, but part of me is not there at all, part of me is thinking about someone who insulted me. I walk into the office, brush past the porter at the desk who is about to say hello, my mind still full of hurt and resentment. I talk on the phone, but am not really concentrating on what I am saying because my mind is besieged by replaying the injustice.

I have become obsessed by a thought and if I am not careful, it will grow out of all proportion and spoil my life. The drive, the porter at the desk, the office, the person at the other end of the telephone are all vague and lifeless. This is how I can shun the world in favor of a shadowy realm of thought.

"Drink a cup of tea," as they say in Zen. Don't think about drinking a cup of tea—just drink it. Taste it. Feel it. Enjoy it. That is experience beyond thought.

A Training?

If Buddhist meditation is reduced to a training course for the purposes of strengthening one's powers of concentration and attaining spiritual goals, then the point of it will be completely missed. One can train oneself to sit, of course, in the full lotus posture without moving even a hair for hours on end, and that will, indeed, improve one's powers of concentration, but the inner eye will not be opened on that account.

Becoming very proficient, sitting beautifully just like a buddha, will impress our friends, perhaps. And if others are not impressed, we shall impress ourselves. We are stalwart "practitioners," never missing a session. Ten, twenty years go by, but what have we achieved? A lovely posture! A serious countenance! An obsession! A lot of pride! And maybe a lot of hidden anxiety too because deep down we will know something is amiss and that, in truth, nothing at all has been achieved.

We need a timetable and a degree of discipline in order to begin, yes, but let us not misuse the props. And let us not count up the sitting hours as credits towards a degree in complete enlightenment to be awarded in later years, or in the next life.

If the motive for meditation is other than waking up, sitting still and staying quiet can be used to remain sound asleep.

The Purpose of Meditation

Meditation is the great antidote to ignorance. It allows us to see ourselves plainly as we are, as if standing before a large clear mirror. Nothing is hidden.

No matter how much we think, debate, or philosophize, we shall never find truth. If we begin with a concept, we shall end up with a concept. And concepts are not truths; they are brain patterns projected on the screen of imagination. This is not to say that truth is not translated into concepts, but the conceptual mind has to be dropped totally before truth is revealed just as it is.

Seeing into the mirror of the mind, therefore, is what meditation is all about.

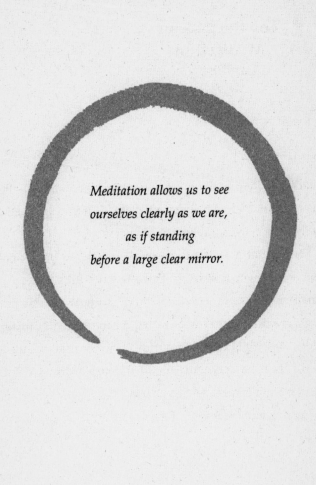

Meditation allows us to see
ourselves clearly as we are,
as if standing
before a large clear mirror.

How to
Meditate

Awareness

If the movements of the body and mental processes are observed intelligently and with an open mind, one soon becomes aware of the mystery in life.

By remaining alert to what is taking place from moment to moment, we discover a side to life that is both liberating and profound. Within that state of being lies the potentiality for unlimited compassion and wisdom. Neither the body, nor the natural thought processes, nor the world in any of its guises enslaves us when we allow thoughts to flow like a stream—coming and going, coming and going—without clinging to any of them.

Be aware of the movements involved in walking. Be aware of standing. Be aware of lying down. Really get into the body; feel being the body; experience all its sensations—pressure, heat, cold, itching, tingling, aching, pain. When sitting, be fully in the sitting; feel the body sitting.

When taking a meal, for example, bring your attention to the smell of the food, to its appearance and texture. Attraction, indifference, repulsion—recognize these sensations as they come into existence. When eating utensils strike the plate, acknowledge their sounds. As food enters the mouth, feel it and taste it fully.

Let the body experience itself. This is the way to be liberated from the body. It's a paradox! To be with the body completely is to be free of it totally. The same is true of the world and the mind. Awareness both in daily life and in formal sitting meditation brings this realization.

Practicing awareness in another sense is practicing recollection. We have to remember to pay attention. Washing, dressing, looking, speaking, feeling, sensing, listening, eating, tasting, touching—it is so easy to forget to live with even the pleasant and beautiful moments in our lives, let alone the unpleasant ones! The tendency is to slip into a separate world of thought, without ever noticing what we are doing. And then we miss the depth of the experience.

Awareness is the practice of staying with all experiences

and impressions as they occur. And by doing this, gradually, one begins to notice how the mind works. It may come as a surprise to discover, for example, that intention is at the root of any action. There is the intention to walk before taking a step, the intention to speak, the intention to work, the intention to lose one's temper before it happens. When the mind decides, the body acts. The body responds, therefore, to impulses in the mind.

Try slowing down a little when you move and then notice intentions as they arise; name them (silently to yourself) and then be aware of and name the actions that follow:

Intending to stand, standing; intending to walk,
walking; intending to raise the arm, raising, and so on.

As we become accustomed to noticing intentions in the mind, we shall be giving ourselves the opportunity to change those intentions. We don't have to lose our tempers if we see the intention there before it has been acted upon; we can let it go, drop it so that it never comes to fruition. We may not want to drop it, of course, but we see that it is our choice. At least we shall be giving ourselves the opportunity of making that choice and of realizing that we are not victims of our own tendencies and previous conditioning; we can change if we wish.

Attending to actions and naming them is merely being aware of normal everyday activities, but in a precise way. The naming should be silent, in the mind, and not spoken out loud.

In the same way, emotional states can be acknowledged for what they are—anxiety, confusion, happiness, sadness, hopefulness, fear . . . How are you now? Happy? Sad? Neither happy nor sad? Be aware of it; say it to yourself. Know the position of the body and know the state of the mind as much as possible throughout the day.

Jealousy, hatred, excitement, bliss, anger, grief, despair—when one of them comes, try to identify the feeling accurately and without attempting to do anything about it. Sensations and emotional states want to live—let them. Then they will want to die. Let them. Give them space and respect, but not energy. This is done simply by being aware; it isn't a complicated process. Try to be open to the new moment that is about to begin.

Powerful thoughts and emotions have a tendency to want to stick; there is something rather attractive about them, even the painful ones. But to let thoughts and feelings go is no great loss—to be aware has something much more powerful to offer.

• Awareness in Everyday Life

Be aware of:
    actions,
    intentions,
    emotional states,
    mental and physical reactions.

Make an effort to remember to be aware.

Let the body be aware of itself.

Let things go—passing thoughts, opinions, and emotional states.

Sitting Meditation

Find a quiet place where you can be totally free of interruptions—a room, if possible, or a small corner of the house. Make it very clear to husband, wife, children, or anyone else living in the house, "This is a time I am not to be disturbed. Questions, telephone messages, and miscellaneous bits of information can wait." Be very clear and firm, otherwise your meditation will be tense and anxious as you sit in wait for a voice calling your name.

If the rest of the family think you are crazy, fine. You are about to embark on an exciting journey and do not wish to be cheated out of it by others' opinions. And don't feel guilty about taking the time for yourself. It's funny how others can become rather jealous of moments one wishes to spend alone. You may well be accused of being selfish, irresponsible in your consideration of others, and of wanting to escape reality. Don't be put off!

So you are in your quiet room and the door is shut. You may also want to meditate with others. Indeed, group meditation can be encouraging and supportive, and a good atmosphere can develop in a room where a few people are meditating together.

Now a sitting posture is to be adopted. There are several to choose from. Find the one that is most suitable for you. Experiment.

• The Lotus Posture

The traditional lotus posture is the ideal position because it is firm, balanced, and relaxed. However, it is very difficult for adults to adopt without a great deal of practice and effort. Do not force yourself into it.

Sit on a firm padded cushion with your legs stretched out in front. (You may have to experiment with the height of the cushion.) Draw in one foot (say the right), bringing the heel as close to the body as possible. Rest the right knee to the ground. Take hold of the left foot and bring it up onto the

right thigh so that the foot, sole upward, is tucked into the groin. Then let the left knee rest down to the ground. Now bring the right leg out from under the left and let the left knee drop to the ground. Draw the right foot up onto the left thigh, positioning it, as with the left, as close to the groin as possible, and relax the knee to the ground.

Ideally, the position of the legs should be reversed from time to time (one foot and then the other being brought up first—maybe after twenty or thirty minutes of sitting, or simply alternating from one session to the next). This helps to maintain a balance in the body.

• The Half Lotus

Then there is the half lotus, which is also a very good posture.

Sit on a cushion of suitable height. Stretch both legs out in front. Draw in one foot (say the right) and bring the heel as close to the body as possible. Rest the knee to the ground. Take the left foot and draw it up onto the right thigh. Let the knee come to rest on the ground.

Reverse the position at appropriate times, as in the case of the full lotus posture.

• Simple Cross-legged Posture

There is a simple variation of the cross-legged posture that many people find possible without too much difficulty.

Sit on a cushion. Take hold of one foot and draw the heel close in to the body. Take the other foot and pull it as close as possible to the first so that the two feet are touching and the two heels are in line with the middle of the body. Both knees should be on the ground.

Swap the position at appropriate times so that the other foot is drawn close to the body first.

• Kneeling

If sitting cross-legged is unsuitable for you, then you may find it better to kneel. This can be done with the aid of a cushion that you straddle, or with the aid of a specially designed stool with a sloping top.

• Sitting on a chair

For many people, the best way of sitting is on a chair. Use an upright dining chair and sit away from the back so that you do not lean. Tuck the feet under the chair a little so that they are not directly beneath the knees (this will give greater support).

If the chair is too high, place a cushion under the feet. This will prevent the edge of the chair from pressing into the back of the thighs.

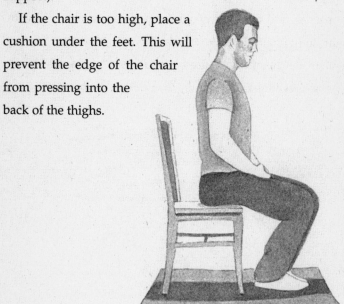

• Alternatives

If none of the postures described here are attainable, find one that is. It may be a matter of lying flat on your back. The important thing is to meditate, and in the final event any position will do.

A certain amount of experimentation may be needed in order to find the right position—one that can be held without too much difficulty for about twenty minutes. You may, of course, want to practice a posture that you would like to be able to adopt while sitting, but cannot yet manage.

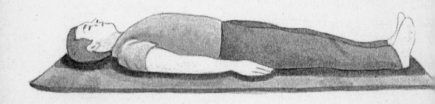

• The Spine

The spine should be erect in whatever posture you have adopted. Then the trunk will be perfectly balanced and the possibility of strain in the back will be eliminated. Such a position can easily be maintained for many hours.

It may be helpful to have someone correct your posture for you at some point, particularly the position of the trunk and back, because what to you feels straight may not be.

The back of the head should be in line with the back of the neck; the head, therefore, tilts forward slightly.

The position of the body needs to be balanced, firm, and relaxed.

• The Eyes

The eyes can be:

Closed completely.

Almost closed, but not tightly, so that the eyelids are relaxed.

Open enough to look down at the floor a foot or so in front of you, without focusing on anything.

• The Hands

The hands can be held palms upward, one on top of the other, loosely in the lap, or with the thumbs held up but not quite touching, as pictured.

Duration

It is important to decide beforehand how long a session is to last, otherwise all the while you will be wondering, Shall I stop now?

Ten minutes is enough initially and can be increased to fifteen or twenty after a few days or weeks.

At the end of some weeks of regular sitting, thirty minutes may feel more appropriate. Experienced meditators tend not to sit for more than an hour or so in any one sitting. You must judge for yourself what feels right.

The duration of the sitting is no mark of progress; it is the quality of each moment that is important. If the sitting becomes an endurance test, it has lost its value and you will be wasting your time. Worse, you will be putting yourself off meditation altogether. Better to sit for a shorter period with enthusiasm and energy than to drag yourself through an hour.

You will need some way of marking the time. Traditionally, burning a stick of incense has been used as a timer. You could do that too, after establishing how long it takes to burn any particular kind of incense. Alternatively, you could use a nice "quiet" alarm clock, or the alarm on your watch if you have one, or a kitchen timer. Glancing at a clock from time to time is possible but can be a distraction.

When to Sit

When is the best time of day to meditate? Some say first thing in the morning, others say last thing at night. You must find out for yourself. The deciding factor may not be the state of your mind, but a busy schedule, or the busy life of your family. The best time may be in the middle of the afternoon when everyone is out, or at dawn when they are all still sleeping and the air is clear, or at ten o'clock at night when the kids are in bed and silence reigns.

It is good to make a time for yourself to meditate; then you don't have to think about it anymore. But try not to become obsessive about the time. I know of people who simply cannot get through the day unless they sit in formal meditation for the specified time, no matter what special circumstances arise. Their meditation takes precedence over everything, even matters that affect others seriously.

You can always postpone your meditation a little, or leave it until the following day; nothing will have been lost. If sitting meditation becomes time-oriented and nothing else, something has gone sadly wrong. Meditation is more than just sitting formally by oneself in a quiet room; it is noticing the condition of one's mind in any circumstance; it is becoming aware of the spontaneous uprising of life in each moment. Sitting in a special way is a form to be used for particular purposes, and a very powerful one if used correctly. But one can become obsessive about the time and the form alone with no regard to the content.

There is no doubt, however, that one must give oneself the conditions for meditation and the space for it in one's life. And it is also a fact that the mind does not really want to face itself at any time and will invent reasons for not doing so. Try to be sensitive to what is going on, so that you do not enslave yourself to an ideal on the one hand, or mindlessly go through the motions by sticking rigidly to form, on the other.

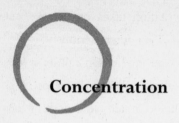

Concentration

You have selected a suitable place in which to meditate, and you have found a comfortable posture in which to sit. The back is straight. The eyes are closed, or half closed. The hands are resting loosely one on top of the other, palms upward, in the lap. The physical side of things is all set. But what is happening in the mind? Is it calm and peaceful? Is it full of expectation? Is it chattering away to itself—imagining, wondering, worrying, planning?

An attempt should now be made to concentrate.

Counting Breaths

Breathe in and count silently to yourself "one." Breathe out and count "one" again. You have now counted one complete breath. On the following inhalation count "two," and "two" on the exhalation. Continue counting for ten full breaths. Then start again at one. There may be some difficulty in retaining full concentration for the time it takes to breathe ten full breaths. The mind will probably wander. If it doesn't, I would be very surprised!

When the mind wanders and the count is lost, simply begin again at one. Should the counting become mechanical, again, go back to one. You may find yourself counting mindlessly beyond ten, and this will be a further indication of loss of concentration. Go back to the beginning again and again. You may find you can hardly reach two before your concentration goes. It doesn't matter. Reaching ten is not the object of the exercise. Trying to do it is the purpose. And in that effort much will be revealed and realized.

You may be surprised at your inability to control the mind for even a very short time. You may be amazed to discover just how much "chatter" goes on, how many images form, how much flitting from subject to subject, or dwelling on one issue there is. You may find that you are unable to simply sit quietly and count a few breaths. The "noise" and "pictures" just won't stop.

Don't become frustrated or depressed on account of this inability to control the mind. You are seeing how the mind works. You are discovering how you work. That is why you are meditating. Be interested in what you are doing and what you discover about yourself. Try to concentrate, but be aware of what happens in that attempt. Forgive yourself if you find your concentration is poor, and continue to make the effort. Make the effort, but without force; try to do it in a gentle way, bringing the mind back to the exercise time and time again. Be patient with yourself. Let yourself be what you are, and try to stay with the counting. Be interested in doing this very simple thing in the moment. This is one-pointed concentration. Be content to count for its own sake. So difficult! So easy!

As the counting takes place to the rhythm of the breath, the mind will be calm and clear, if only for a little while. That moment or two of clarity will be enough to reveal the value of concentration. Worrying, hoping, dreaming, and wishing cannot occupy a space already filled with the counting of breaths. This is a simple revelation that has a deep significance, to be contemplated and fully realized. Just by concentrating in this uncomplicated way, one can come away from, or dissolve, a negative mind state, even if it is only for a moment.

After a while, a degree of concentration and calmness will begin to manifest itself and develop. It is impossible to say how long this will take. For some it may be almost immediate; for others it may take weeks or months, or creep upon them imperceptibly over a longer period of time.

Then, when the time is right, the exercise can be dispensed with. But you must be honest with yourself. Is it time to leave this exercise? Has it served its purpose? There is no point in waiting for perfection! You may never count ten breaths without faltering. It is enough to establish just some concentration, and to experience just some degree of clarity and calmness. If you wait for perfection—an uninterrupted flow of ten counts over and over again for twenty minutes or so—you may wait for a very long time! Move on when you genuinely feel it is time. Experiment if you like; you can always return to this exercise again in the future if you feel you need to. It is all a question of finding that balance between moving too fast and not moving at all.

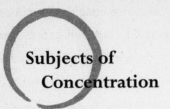

Subjects of
Concentration

Counting breaths is practiced by silently making words to mark off a physical action. The breath is observed and a word is formed. This is concentrating with the aid of thought.

These next exercises are also related to the breathing process, but from a slightly different perspective.

There are many variations on concentrating on the breathing process, but I will list just three. Only one of them is to be used—it doesn't matter which. They are all of equal value, so there is no question of progressing from one to the other. Yet you may wish to try them all out as time goes by in order to see which fits the best. Finally, however, decide on one and stick to that as your practice.

1. Concentrate on the length of breaths taken. Is it a long, deep breath? Is it a short breath? Or is it neither long nor short?

2. Concentrate on the warm and cool sensations in the nostrils as the air flows through while breathing in (cool) and breathing out (warm).

3. Concentrate on the rise and fall of the abdomen (approximately three finger-widths below the navel) while breathing in (rising) and breathing out (falling).

Breathing is a continuous process while one is alive and, for that reason, is a very convenient subject on which to meditate. An important point to remember, however, is that observing the breath is not an exercise in breathing; it is an exercise in observation. Please do not exaggerate or alter the breathing pattern. Simply breathe naturally and become conscious of it.

Alternative Subjects
of Concentration

Sometimes people have difficulty with concentrating on the breath because as soon as they do so, it becomes strained and awkward. Basically, the breathing pattern relates to the state of the mind. When the mind is anxious, the breath will be tense and irregular too. When the mind is calm, the breath will flow evenly and gently, and may become almost imperceptible.

If, after much perseverance, one really cannot get along with watching the breath as a subject, then choose something else. Sound is a good alternative. Even in the quietest places, sounds will be heard—birds, the wind, a train, a plane, the central heating system, and so on, or (when one becomes conscious of it) the sound of silence.

It is better, of course, not to have to listen to someone

else's sound equipment when meditating, so try to avoid it altogether. But if it should happen to invade your quiet space suddenly, then don't reject it either, at least for the duration of that session. Observe the sound as sound without getting drawn into the content of it, and without judging it as pleasant or unpleasant, or right or wrong. This, too, can be a very valuable exercise.

Alternatives to watching the breath are meditating on a flowing stream or the flame of a candle. But there aren't many people who can sit by a flowing stream very often, and staring at the flame of a candle can damage the eyes. So these are not ideal on a long-term basis.

Static objects—an ornament, a flower, the floor, the wall, and so forth—generally are not good subjects. It is all too easy to think while staring at something static, and not realize it. This is why moving objects are better. Movement needs constant attention for it to be followed.

Watch and Note
Without Judging

Now you have chosen a new subject on which to concentrate. Sit in the formal posture, relax into it as much as you can without slumping down, and just breathe. Feel the body sitting and breathing. Nothing else matters.

Now take up the exercise you have chosen from the three listed in "Subjects of Concentration." Supposing you have decided that the rise and fall of the abdomen will be your main object, go to that area now and name the actions that are taking place. The physical movements may be very gentle and subtle, almost imperceptible. It doesn't matter. Don't increase them in an attempt to make them easier to follow. Feel the rise and fall, and say the words silently to yourself, "Rising, falling, rising, falling," as the abdomen moves.

Make sure the words coincide with the actions and let the breath flow naturally.

The rise and fall movements will not be continuous because the breathing is not a continuous process of inhalation/exhalation. There will be rest periods in between. Be equally aware of the gaps and the whole body in contact with the floor and the cushion, or the chair, at these times, and say "sitting" to denote the experience. "Rising, falling, sitting, rising, falling, sitting . . ."

Watch and note without judging. "Good," "bad," "right," "wrong"—these evaluations do not apply to the purity of what is taking place now, about which nothing need be said. When the attention wanders, note it and form the word in the mind—"thinking." Be fully aware that you have been thinking and that it has drawn you away from concentrating on the rise and fall of the abdomen. Take time to fully appreciate what has happened: "Thinking, thinking, thinking." Then go back to the main subject of meditation again: "Rising, falling . . ."

Do not reject thought, sound, sensation, passion, or anything that arises in meditation. Accept it all. Acknowledge it, name it, feel it, and then redirect the attention back to the rise and fall of the abdomen (or whatever the main object of the concentration is). A period of sitting meditation may go something like this:

Rising (of the abdomen), falling, sitting, rising, falling, sitting, rising, falling, aching (of, say, the knee or ankle), aching, aching, aching (and then return to the main subject again), rising, falling (the mind wanders), dreaming, dreaming, dreaming, rising, falling, sitting, rising, itching, itching, itching, rising, falling, wanting to swallow, intending to swallow, swallowing, rising, falling, sitting, thinking, thinking, thinking, rising, falling, pain, pain, pain, wanting to move, rising, falling . . .

Make the meditation subject the center of your gravity, as it were. And whenever you find yourself dreaming about what you are going to have for lunch, or about meeting an old friend in town, stop. Come back to yourself, to where you are and to what you are doing. Acknowledge the truth of the moment and say to yourself, "Dreaming, dreaming, dreaming" (or "planning," or "wanting," or whatever it is that has been occupying you for the last few moments), and go home again to the subject of concentration.

Try to maintain your sitting posture without moving. The

idea is that the living moment can display itself, fulfill itself, only against an intelligent and sensitive stillness, without interference or interruption. For this, not only discursive thinking, but the body also should be inactive. Occasionally, however, particularly in the early days of meditation, an irritation or an ache can become intolerable. Make the decision to relieve the discomfort by moving or scratching the area in question. Then, slowly and mindfully do something about it, acknowledging each and every action as it takes place. "Moving, moving, moving," as the hand, say, moves to the itch, "scratching, scratching, scratching," as the hand slowly scratches the itch, and then, "moving, moving, moving," as the hand returns just as slowly to its original place. Finally, when the whole operation is completed, "Rising, falling, sitting, rising . . ."

Keep up the naming process until the mind wanders less and less, and then leave the naming alone; it will have served its purpose.

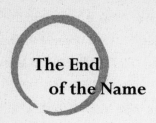

The End
of the Name

All aids to meditation must be dropped at the appropriate time, otherwise they will become too familiar, too comfortable, and no longer of any value. Be ready to drop the naming when the time is ripe.

In the beginning naming is a powerful way of reminding the mind not to produce thoughts beyond what is happening, but it is still a thought-producing activity. As such, it sustains the false notion of a self—"me" watching and naming "it," the body. The rise and fall of the abdomen and the knowing of the rise and fall is not attributable to a self. The sound and the observer of it do not involve a "me" doing it. It is time to see that now.

Observe the rise and fall of the abdomen without thinking about it. Be totally at one with it. As the body moves, be the movement. Do not say to yourself, "This is me sitting here now being aware of my breathing." Do not observe the rise and fall and produce the words "rise" and "fall." Become one with the breathing.

Recognize all that comes, see it for what it is, but do it without labelling it and making a story out of it.

Feel the lightness rushing through the mind and body. Feel the freedom.

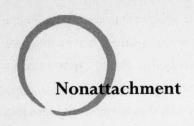

Nonattachment

Be aware of the breathing (the rise and fall) and be aware of whatever else passes by—a sense, a feeling, a thought, a smell, a sound. Let the mind open. Try not to become involved in thoughts.

There are no intrusions or disturbances for one who is really meditating. If you are drawn away from the main point of concentration by a sound, or an ache, or a moment of despair, or a simple thought, and feel it is an intrusion into your special world of meditation, then frustration or anger will surely arise as a result. Be aware of that attitude and any accompanying frustration. Acknowledge the experiences as they arise. They are the reality of the moment.

There is no need to be disappointed or annoyed about being drawn away from the main subject of meditation. No crime has been committed. Accept whatever comes; be prepared to welcome it even. Then everything will be the meditation itself and will be regarded as an opportunity for change. This is turning the negative into the positive.

The mind, life itself, is crushed by clinging and rejecting. Clinging and rejecting are two sides of the same coin. They are the forceful, even violent, activities of the ego-centered aspect of this phenomenon I call "me." Have the courage to let a thought slip by and not chase after it. Not clinging to thought, not rejecting it, the mind will open to a natural awareness. And awareness moves where life moves, not where hopes, fears, and wishes move. Come away from the wandering dreamy mind into the reality of the moment and cling to nothing. Be totally free.

This possibility exists for you, for me, and for anyone who has the courage to trust life, forego the past, and allow the moment to be itself.

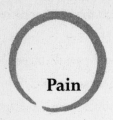

Pain

We reject certain sensations; we dislike them; we don't want them. Annoyance, impatience, anxiety, or resentment arise as a result of rejecting sensations. In an attempt to keep suffering at bay, therefore, greater suffering is experienced. If pain springs up while meditating, maybe in the knee or ankle, try to give it space in your consciousness without fear or ill will. Attend to the pain very carefully and observe it impersonally as though it belonged to someone else; simply let it be.

After a moment or two the pain may subside (pain usually comes in waves), in which case go back to the rise and fall. On the other hand, the pain may increase. If it does and becomes intolerable, then there is no point in struggling under the weight of it. Mindfully reposition the body and continue concentrating on the breath.

Bearable pain, however, can be a very useful subject on which to meditate. An ache, a pain, an itch has life. Relax and let it live. It will not survive forever; nothing does. And here is an opportunity to look at pain, something you may normally regard as unpleasant, without regarding it as anything at all. Then you will experience pain without suffering.

Joy and bliss may also spring up and pervade one's being in meditation. This is a result of meditating on the body and not attaching to anything. Continue to be aware. Let the sensations come and go without interference. If you identify with bliss and indulge in it, grasping will enter into the situation and there will be a sense of loss and disappointment when the sensation departs, with an added feeling or desire for recreating it.

Nonattachment to all sensations—pleasant or unpleasant—is the route to happiness.

Walking Meditation

Walking is a wonderful way of meditating. It brings one to the point of realizing that meditation does not depend upon the position of the body.

Walking meditation puts sitting meditation into motion. This can break down misconceptions about meditation being something that can take place only in perfect stillness.

Freedom from form, feelings, perceptions, impulses, and any type of consciousness—this little bundle called "me"—can be experienced at any time by engaging in the business at hand in a meditative way, whether it be the rise and fall of the abdomen or the placing of one foot in front of the other in walking meditation.

Stand upright and perfectly still.

Allow your arms to hang loosely by your sides or as pictured.

Look at the ground far enough ahead to see where you are going, but don't study what you see.

Concentrate on the body, the whole body, standing.

Notice the intention to raise one foot.

Place your attention on that foot.

Raise the foot a little and momentarily hold it there.

Notice the intention to move the foot forward.

Move it forward and hold it for a moment just above the ground.

Notice the intention to place the foot to the ground.

Place it to the ground.

Now repeat the process with the other foot.

Name what is happening to you in the way that you do, initially, in the sitting practice: "Intending to raise, raising; intending to move, moving; intending to place, placing . . ." Continue walking for, say, fifteen steps, or until there is no more floor space. If the exercise takes place outside, find a suitable spot and limit the distance to about thirty steps, otherwise you could find yourself enjoying a lovely walk somewhere, but not practicing what you had set out to do.

At the end of the stretch of floor or path, stand for a moment or two. Be aware of the whole body standing. Be aware of the intention to turn. Notice that intention. And then turn slowly until you are facing the opposite direction. Now continue, walking back again.

Practice walking up and down slowly for ten or twenty minutes.

In sitting meditation one point only is focused upon while acknowledging whatever else happens to arise. In walking meditation, however, many movements are observed. Each is taken slowly and deliberately and concentrated upon. Whenever concentration is lost, stand for a moment, re-establish the concentration, and then continue. There is no need to stop on account of every fleeting thought that passes the clear space of your mind, however. Spontaneous thoughts, sounds, smells, the wind in your face, the pressure under your feet will appear and disappear in your consciousness. Let them come and go as they please. Only if you become completely absorbed into some mind state do you need to stop, allow the concentration to return to the body, and continue again.

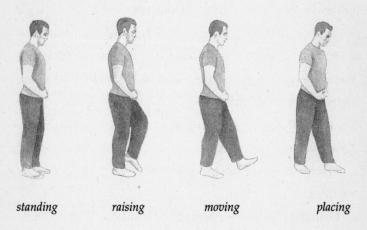

standing   raising   moving   placing

"Standing, standing, standing; intending to raise (the foot), raising; intending to move (the foot), moving; intending to place (the foot to the ground), placing; intending to raise, raising; intending to move, moving . . ."

raising   moving   placing

Just before turning to walk back again, stand for a moment: "Standing, standing, standing; intending to turn, turning, turning, turning; standing, standing, standing; intending to raise, raising . . ."

standing   turning   turning

turning   standing   raising

As with the other practices, naming the movements should be dropped in due course, so that you become aware solely of walking.

In Review

● **Sitting Meditation**

Find a quiet place.

Set a time for the duration of the sitting.

Adopt a suitable sitting posture:
cross-legged;
kneeling with a cushion or stool;
on a chair.

Eyes half or fully closed.

Rest hands loosely in the lap (palms upward, one on top of the other).

• Counting Breaths

Inhale—"one"; exhale—"one";
inhale—"two"; exhale—"two" . . .
and so on up to ten.

If concentration is lost, begin again at one.

• Subjects of Concentration

Choose one of the following:

1. Concentrate on the length of each breath—long, short, or neither long nor short.

2. Concentrate on the warm and cool air flowing through the nostrils (inhalation—cool; exhalation—warm).

3. Concentrate on the rise and fall of the abdomen (a point approximately three finger-widths below the navel).

Take up one of the above subjects. Acknowledge thoughts, feelings, and sensations as they arise. Return to the main subject whenever possible.

• Walking Meditation

Find a stretch of floor upon which you can take at least eight consecutive steps in a straight line (fifteen would be better) or locate a secluded spot in the open.

Set a time for the exercise (ten or twenty minutes).

The arms are to hang loosely by one's sides.

Stand perfectly still.

Lower the eyes to the ground just ahead.

Name the actions initially and then, when the inclination to stay with whatever is happening in the moment is greater than the tendency to drift off into dreams, imaginings, and thoughts of the past or the future, discontinue the naming and be aware of what is happening in a more immediate and direct way.

Just Sit

There will come a time in meditation when any subject of concentration, the rise and fall of the abdomen, for example, will become more of a hindrance than a help in staying with the reality of the moment. How long will this take? That is impossible to say.

But when there is total acceptance of the moment, all predetermined objects of concentration can and should be dispensed with because that is when the eyes of the mind are wide open. The body breathes; life is the way it is; no complications, no self, no other, no time, no birth, no death, no eternity, no annihilation, no one to breathe, no one to worry. Here—just sitting.

Let go of all subjects of concentration and just sit. Thoughts will come and go, of course, as well as feelings and sensations, but behind those natural uprisings, a deep clarity of mind, an intense calmness and great energy will extend throughout one's being and throughout the whole field of consciousness. Sitting in meditation, being open to what comes, without thought-commentary, without feeling the need to tell yourself, "That's the wind blowing in the trees"; "That's a train passing"; "That's the smell of toast"; "That's a pain in my right knee"; "That's a bird singing"; you just know these things before the voice of the mind speaks, before images are made.

The echo of, "Oh, what a beautiful sunset," in our minds removes us from the beauty. The, "Oh, how dreadful it is that they suffer so much," removes us from a deep inner connection with those beings. The essence of what we are knows what is going on without having it explained or repeated in code. In fact, only the essence of mind knows; nothing else does.

In awareness one sees and knows with a mind free of emotions, greed, hatred, and delusion. It isn't that one loses the power to think, of course, and plan, and remember past events. It's just that one is moved by what one experiences rather than by what one thinks about.

There is a famous saying by a Zen master, "When hungry,

eat. When thirsty, drink. When tired, sleep." To live in a simple, direct way, without cluttering up the mind with wanting things, hating things, judging, taking too much, worrying, or doubting is a wonderful experience of genuine happiness. And it's ours for the taking.

It is important to be sensible when formulating a program for yourself from the exercises in this book; they are suggestions only, hints. You must find your own way, otherwise it will be like wearing someone else's coat which doesn't fit properly. Meditate freely.

Living
Truth

The Unborn

In meditation all things are seen to be impermanent—they come and they go. And whatever comes and goes cannot be regarded as "me," a self. But who is it that knows this? Who knows the birth and death of a sound . . . a sensation . . . a dream? Sound itself doesn't know sound. Sensation doesn't know itself. Something else does that. Is it thought, or the thinking mind? I have already discovered through meditation that thoughts are nothing but mental creations—memories, hopes, dreams, fears. They are forms that have been produced and are also known by something other than themselves.

A sound, a thought, a sensation, a dream—these are all born into existence and they all die. They are all born, but that which experiences whatever has been born—is that born? How can it be? This is the same as asking, "Who am I?" And that is a good question too.

Many people understand instinctively that they are more than just flesh and blood and mental processes, yet they cannot make any sense of it intellectually and fail to recognize it on a conscious level.

It is easy to see how thoughts, sensations, and whatever else is perceived arise and pass away, and how the body changes. This arising and passing away is birth and death. The unborn, that which is aware of this arising and passing away, however, does not come into being and does not cease to be.

Feel the Sensation

There is incredible beauty in moving the body, touching things, picking them up, carrying them from place to place, washing dishes, polishing wood and metal, placing ink on paper, smoothing the creases with an iron, looking at some-one openly.

It is extraordinary, but even the simplest of tasks embod-ies the greatest spiritual happiness when performed calmly and with a quiet mind. When nothing is yearned for we are free to enjoy what we do, free to see the patterns, to hear the music in all things.

"But," you may say, "I haven't got the time; I have to do

things in such a rush—the house, the kids, the job. I haven't got time to see the incredible beauty in washing the pots. Have you seen that pile over there?"

How is one able to do a job calmly and in one's own time when there are so many things to do? Pay full attention to what you are doing and let the body move. It will be the greatest of joys. Don't do a job just to get it done even if you have to rush; that's a waste! Do it with all of your being. Do it for its own sake and know time—the time to begin, the time to end, the time to wait, the time to go.

Stretch out your hand and touch an object very gently and with great sensitivity. Feel the sensation in your hand and arm and the whole of your body. Let the division between you and the things you touch disappear. Learn to love movement and contact, sound and color.

Things turn out badly sometimes. Living is a precarious business; most people are crushed by it at some point in their lives, if not all of their lives. They think pleasure is good and pain is bad. Recognize the true self and the nature of this moment, and realize there is nothing to crush.

There is a very easy pattern to life. If you stay with the moment, there is just enough time to do what needs to be done, just enough materials to complete the job as far as it needs completing. And if the time has run out and panic sets in, well, that can be interesting too. Smile a little. Not every demand for your attention needs to be gratified. Not every letter needs a reply. Not every offer should be accepted. The body goes to what is right, does what is right. If truth is your purpose, the mind will inevitably incline towards it.

Be aware of the breath entering and leaving the body. Look at the rise and fall of the abdomen. Look at the body walking in silence. Look at others walking by. Listen without desire. Look at the mind. Look at pleasure. Look at pain. Open the inner eye and see this very moment, now. Sense life, smell it, taste it, listen to it directly with the very core of your being. The mundane will become profound.

If boredom comes, brush it aside; don't attach to it. It is another condition of the mind that distorts the truth. The moment is not dull and boring; only the mind makes it so. If pain comes, let it be. There is something painless in the heart of being and the essence of the moment. If agitation comes, let it settle. Trying to force calmness will only create further agitation. In a quieter moment take the opportunity to return to the source of your being.

There can be no end to insight, so many are the ways of experiencing the same thing. As one draws closer to an object, it changes its form. There is no need to go anywhere or to do anything to plumb the depths of the universe and one's own being.

Enjoy washing that pile of pots!

The Way

Happiness cannot be forced into existence, nor can it be forced out of it, but it can be held in abeyance. That is what we do when we hang on to things and people and ideas in our minds and refuse to let them go. The mind becomes blocked and the way is dammed up.

Being alert, observing the movements of the mind and body in daily life, noticing what is taking place—as opposed to what one wishes would take place, or what one fears might take place, or what one grieves over as having already taken place—is a way of life that is completely free of all self-imposed restrictions and conflicting states of mind. Wisdom and compassion will be allowed to function freely under these circumstances.

Views, speech, ways of living, mindfulness, and concentration are unhindered by greed, guilt, hatred, carelessness, complacency, and fear when divisions are seen to be arbitrary and there is no sense of "This is me"; "that is you."

When the way ahead is open and clear and one has the goodwill, light-heartedness, and courage to tread it, the past and the future melt into nothingness, life is lived from the center of one's being, and the self becomes as meaningful as the blue sky, the green fields, the flowing rivers, the littered streets, the hustling crowds, the filth, and the beauty.

When one follows what is right according to one's heart and good sense, when wisdom and compassion become real, not contrived, the way of heaven manifests beneath one's feet. That is the way of liberation from suffering and the realization of genuine happiness.